Talyllyn Railway Reco

First published in 2011

British Library Cataloguing in Publication Data

A catalogue record for this book is available
from the British Library.

ISBN 978 1 85794 370 2

Silver Link Publishing Ltd
The Trundle
Ringstead Road
Great Addington
Kettering
Northants NN14 4BW

Tel/Fax: 01536 330588
email: sales@nostalgiacollection.com
Website: www.nostalgiacollection.com

Printed and bound in the Czech Republic

Contents

This book is dedicated to all Talyllyn Railway
volunteers, past, present and future.

Frontispiece **DOLGOCH FALLS:** A superb
night shot of No 2 *Dolgoch* at Dolgoch Falls
station with a photographic special *David
Mitchell*

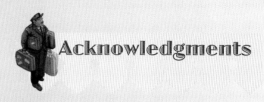

Acknowledgments

No book of this kind is possible without the
photographs! Therefore I am extremely grateful
to all the photographers – some unknown
because their photographs came from the TR
collection – whose work has been used. I owe
a particular debt of gratitude to David Mitchell,
a long-standing TR volunteer who, as you will
see from the captions, has provided most of
the photographs. I am also grateful to Matthew
Wear for typing the captions and to Celia
Adams and Lawrie Bowles (both long-standing
volunteers) for proofreading. Last, but by no
mean least, I want to thank the volunteers on
the Talyllyn Railway who make all this possible
by their dedication to and support of the
railway. This small book is a tribute to them
for their skills and for providing those skills
so readily to ensure that the Talyllyn Railway
is there for generations to come. I have been
a volunteer for 28 years and my only regret is
that I didn't start as a teenager as my elder son,
Justin, did!

Introduction

The idea for this book came from a discussion I had with Peter Townsend of Silver Link Publishing Ltd about the possibility of marking the 60th anniversary of the Talyllyn Railway Preservation Society, founded in October 1950. The TR was the first preserved steam railway in the world and the first to be operated by volunteers. The first train ran from Wharf to Rhydyronen on 14 May 1951, now marked every year as 'Founders Day'.

Peter suggested that a book about the TR in the 'Recollections' series would be a good idea. It is being published after 60 years operation of the Talyllyn Railway by the Preservation Society and marks a wonderful achievement by the volunteers over that time, and long may it continue.

However the continued operation of the TR depends on a steady supply of new volunteers. We currently have a dedicated band of volunteers, including many young people, but we are always on the look-out for more.

I hope that readers will be encouraged to offer their services. If they do, they will find it extremely rewarding and meet new friends who share a common interest.

Come and join us, you will not be disappointed!

Nigel Adams

TYWYN WHARF: Loco No 1 *Talyllyn* waits at Wharf station. *TR collection*

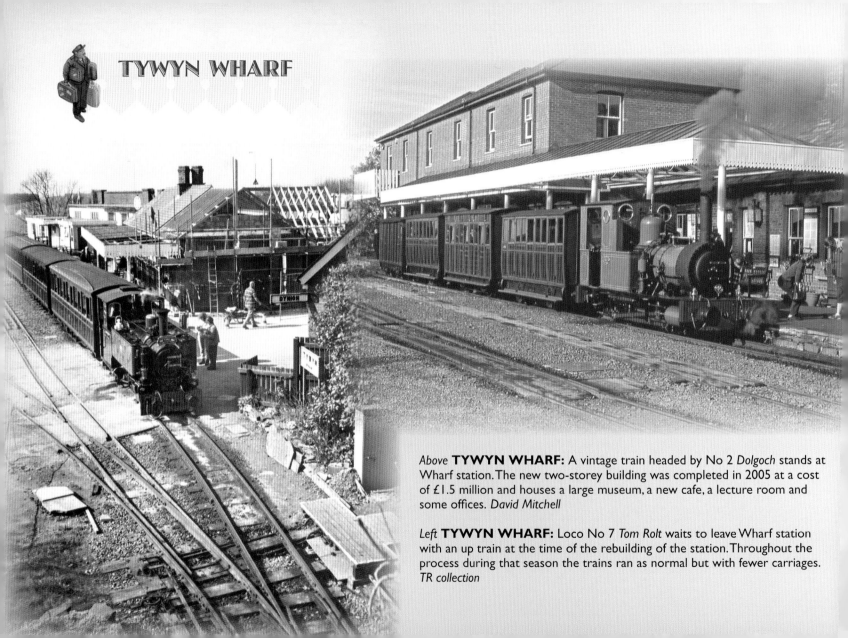

TYWYN WHARF

Above **TYWYN WHARF:** A vintage train headed by No 2 *Dolgoch* stands at Wharf station. The new two-storey building was completed in 2005 at a cost of £1.5 million and houses a large museum, a new cafe, a lecture room and some offices. *David Mitchell*

Left **TYWYN WHARF:** Loco No 7 *Tom Rolt* waits to leave Wharf station with an up train at the time of the rebuilding of the station. Throughout the process during that season the trains ran as normal but with fewer carriages. *TR collection*

TYWYN WHARF YARD: No 1 *Talyllyn* arrives in Wharf yard on 6 October 2010 with one of the original coaches and the original guard's van. This train was specially marshalled with the van at the rear to commemorate the last 'Haydn Jones train' in 1950. *David Mitchell*

TYWYN WHARF CUTTING: Loco No 4, masquerading as *Peter Sam*, heads a train up Wharf Cutting. TR locos normally face 'chimney first' in the up direction, as here, but occasionally a loco is turned for photographic purposes. *TR collection*

TYWYN WHARF YARD: No 7 *Tom Rolt* takes water at Wharf station on 19 January 2009. There is good detail in this photograph for the railway modeller – note the fire irons hanging on the water tower and the working gas lamp. *David Mitchell*

PENDRE: Pendre station in the 1940s.
Author's collection

PENDRE This photograph taken at Pendre by John Slater in the late 1950s shows a view that has changed out of all recognition as the field between the railway and the houses in Frankwell Street has since had houses built on it. *Author's collection*

PENDRE On 21 October 2006 Blockman (and Chief Signalling Inspector) Ian Grayston presides over a crossing at Pendre as he waits to exchange tokens with Driver Andy Young on the Wharf-bound train. Loco No 2 *Dolgoch* waits with an up train in the loop. *David Mitchell*

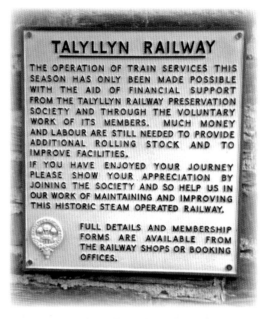

TALYLLYN RAILWAY

THE OPERATION OF TRAIN SERVICES THIS SEASON HAS ONLY BEEN MADE POSSIBLE WITH THE AID OF FINANCIAL SUPPORT FROM THE TALYLLYN RAILWAY PRESERVATION SOCIETY AND THROUGH THE VOLUNTARY WORK OF ITS MEMBERS. MUCH MONEY AND LABOUR ARE STILL NEEDED TO PROVIDE ADDITIONAL ROLLING STOCK AND TO IMPROVE FACILITIES.

IF YOU HAVE ENJOYED YOUR JOURNEY PLEASE SHOW YOUR APPRECIATION BY JOINING THE SOCIETY AND SO HELP US IN OUR WORK OF MAINTAINING AND IMPROVING THIS HISTORIC STEAM OPERATED RAILWAY.

FULL DETAILS AND MEMBERSHIP FORMS ARE AVAILABLE FROM THE RAILWAY SHOPS OR BOOKING OFFICES.

Y CHWARELWR THE QUARRYMAN

PENDRE: Driver John Robinson prepares to exchange tokens with an unknown blockman at Pendre as *Peter Sam* (really No 4 *Edward Thomas*) passes with an up train. No 1 *Talyllyn* is standing in the loop with a down train. When the up train has passed through, the blockman will set the road for the loop, obtain the necessary token and give it to the driver of No 1 so that his train can depart for Wharf. *David Mitchell, TR collection*

Below **PENDRE YARD:** In 1983 the TR had a loco from the Corris Railway on loan for a period. It was named *Alan Meaden* and is seen here on 27 July with a down train passing through Pendre yard with No 3 (minus a name) and the Corris coach (No 17) standing on the loop. *The late Phil Guest*

Right **PENDRE:YARD:** No 3 *Sir Haydn*, named after Sir Henry Haydn Jones, the Liberal MP for Merioneth who bought the TR in 1910 and kept it running until his death in 1950, stands outside Pendre loco shed masquerading as *Sir Handel* with an injured face. Driver Roy Smith takes an up train past the shed with No 1 *Talyllyn. TR collection*

Right **Nr. RHYDYRONEN:** The late Maurice Wilson leans out of the cab of loco No 3 on 23 June 1995 on an early-morning photographic special; the author was the guard. The train left Pendre at 7.00am to get the photographic benefits of the rising sun on that glorious June day. *Robert Morland*

Below **PENDRE YARD:** Chief Executive Dave Scotson is also a driver and a blockman when he can find the time! Previously the Engineering Manager, he is seen here pushing round hard-to-turn loco No 6 *Douglas* outside the north carriage shed at Pendre. *TR collection*

HENDY HALT: A view up the Fathew Valley from the fireman's side of cab of No 1 *Talyllyn* as it approaches Hendy Halt, between Pendre and Rhydyronen. *David Mitchell*

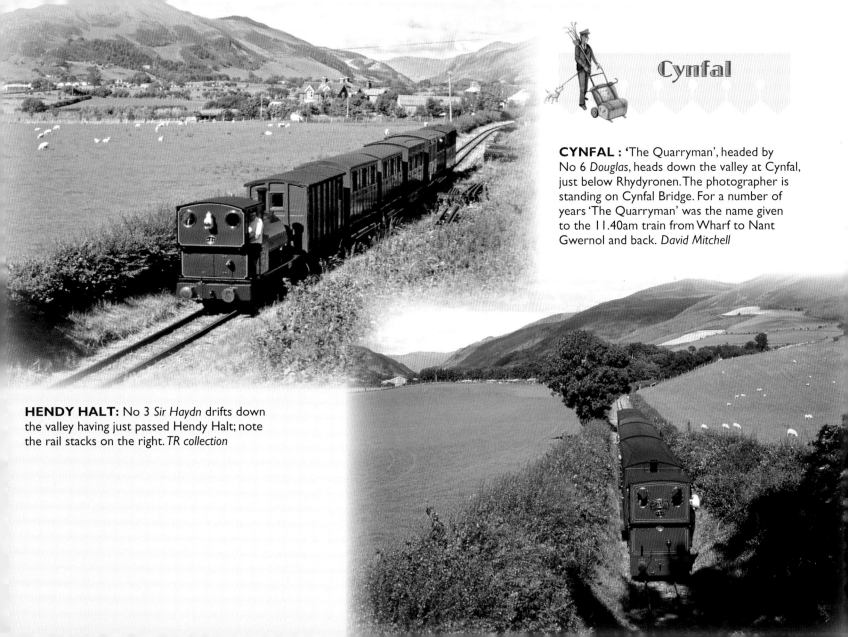

Cynfal

CYNFAL : 'The Quarryman', headed by No 6 *Douglas*, heads down the valley at Cynfal, just below Rhydyronen. The photographer is standing on Cynfal Bridge. For a number of years 'The Quarryman' was the name given to the 11.40am train from Wharf to Nant Gwernol and back. *David Mitchell*

HENDY HALT: No 3 *Sir Haydn* drifts down the valley having just passed Hendy Halt; note the rail stacks on the right. *TR collection*

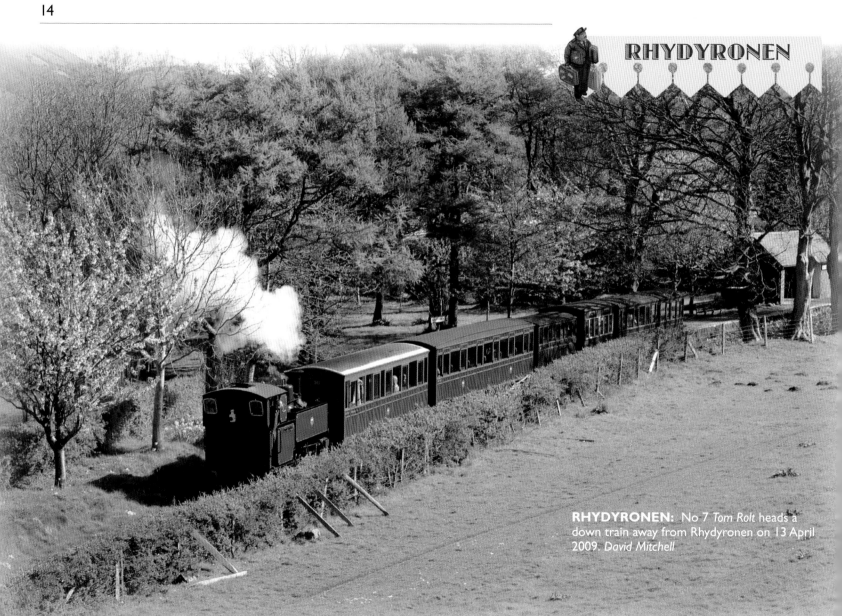

RHYDYRONEN

RHYDYRONEN: No 7 *Tom Rolt* heads a down train away from Rhydyronen on 13 April 2009. *David Mitchell*

Above **RHYDYRONEN:** Driver Mike Green brings a three-coach train into Rhydyronen with loco No 4 *Edward Thomas* on 5 March 2010. This is a popular station in the peak season due to the nearby Tynllwyn Caravan and Camping Park. *David Mitchell*

Right **RHYDYRONEN:** Driver Rob Frost on No 7 *Tom Rolt* brings a special train into Rhydyronen on Good Friday 2010. Note the marvellous array of flowers – these are mainly daffodils but there are also primroses and celandines in the spring. *Paul Gunn*

Top right **RHYDYRONEN:** Driver Martin Fuller is aboard No 2 *Dolgoch* at Rhydyronen at the head of a vintage train on 5 March 5 2008, while Guard Noel Williams shelters from the cold in the station building. *David Mitchell*

Left **RHYDYRONEN:** Fireman Alex Eyres (at the regulator) and Driver David Jones bring No 1 *Talyllyn* (minus its cab) under Rhydyronen bridge with a photographic special on 17 March 2007. The station platform and name board are just visible under the bridge. *David Mitchell*

Below **RHYDYRONEN:** No 6 *Douglas*, masquerading as *Duncan*, which children love, passes Tynllwyn Caravan and Camping site as it leaves Rhydyronen with an up train. *David Mitchell*

Nr **RHYDYRONEN (BRYNERWEST):** A photographic special heads up the valley at Brynerwest on 4 March 2008. The photographers travel in a brake-van and a coach, which are detached from the train. Then they go into one of the fields (with the farmer's permission!) and the train does as many run-pasts as required until they are happy with the photographs they have taken. They then return to the coach and brake-van, which are recoupled to the train to travel on to the next location. *David Mitchell*

RHYDYRONEN: This cast plate says it all. *Sara Eade, TR collection*

Brynglas

BRYNGLAS: For many years on a Tuesday evening in August the local Gardening Club in Tywyn has run 'The Floral Train', seen here approaching Brynglas complete with its floral decorations.
Terry Eyres, TR collection

Right **BRYNGLAS:** Hauling a photographic special train at Brynglas is No 2 *Dolgoch*, and the vintage Morris Minor belongs to Jonathan and Lis Mann, who both volunteer on the TR although they live in Cornwall, as the sticker on the left-hand side of the rear window shows! *David Mitchell*

Below **BRYNGLAS:** Driver Gareth Jones is at the regulator of loco No 1 *Talyllyn* as his train approaches the up whistle board at Brynglas on 27 July 2008 *David Mitchell*

Below **BRYNGLAS:** Total devastation! On the evening of 10 June 1993 a torrential rainstorm swept rubbish and debris down off the hills at Brynglas, totally blocking the track. The next day trains did not run. This photograph was taken on Saturday the 12th as the initial clearing up was coming to an end. The first passenger train departed from Wharf at 2.25pm and had to run 'wrong road' through the loop with clipped points at the west end because the main line had been washed away. *Author*

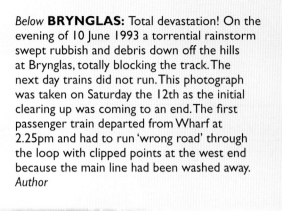

Above **BRYNGLAS:** The damage repaired, No 1 *Talyllyn* stands in Brynglas loop with a photographic special slate wagon train. The driver is the late Phil Guest, the fireman (seen looking out) is Alex Eyres, and the author (seen oiling up) is the guard. *Chris Worley, TR collection*

BRYNGLAS: A lovely evening shot of loco No 1 *Talyllyn* drifting down the bank just above Brynglas. The fireman is driving under instruction, with Driver Roy Smith on the fireman's side. *David Mitchell*

BRYNGLAS: No 2 *Dolgoch* stands with an up train in Brynglas loop while a down train, headed by *Tom Rolt* (No 7), passes on 13 April 2010. The fireman exchanges a few words with the up train driver while the down train guard watches his train. When the down train has cleared the bottom end of the loop, the blockman will reset the points and give a green flag to the up train, then stand on the road crossing ready to give the fireman the token for the Brynglas-Quarry Siding section of the line. *David Mitchell*

Dolgoch Falls

Right **DOLGOCH FALLS:** Driver Bill Heynes is on loco No 2 *Dolgoch* with 'The Quarryman' as it passes through the woods just below Dolgoch. *David Mitchell*

Opposite inset **DOLGOCH FALLS:** Martin Fuller and Martin Lester head out of Dolgoch Falls station over the viaduct with loco No 4 *Edward Thomas* and a down train. *David Mitchell*

Opposite main picture **DOLGOCH FALLS:** No 1 *Talyllyn* heads its train over the viaduct into Dolgoch Falls station on 17 March 2010. The viaduct is more than 60 feet above the footpath, and there are beautiful walks here to the bottom, middle and top falls. *David Mitchell*

DOLGOCH FALLS: Looking back in time, No 4 *Edward Thomas*, fitted with a Giesl ejector, is filled with water at Dolgoch Falls station on 9 August 1961. *Norman Jones, TR collection*

DOLGOCH FALLS: No 4 *Edward Thomas* is seen again in modern times on a down train, taking water from the original water tower at Dolgoch. Unusually the loco is chimney first in the down direction. Fireman Andrew Thomas has set up the wooden chute and controls the flow of the water by pulling on the chain, while off-duty volunteer Philip Sayers watches with interest. *David Mitchell*

DOLGOCH FALLS: Some TR volunteers and visitors from the Gwynedd Archives Office at Dolgellau are seen at Dolgoch Falls station on 11 July 2010, on a special train to mark the accreditation of the new museum at Wharf. *David Mitchell*

DOLGOCH FALLS: A vintage train heads up the valley in Dolgoch Woods on 15 March 2010. *David Mitchell*

DOLGOCH FALLS: A lovely snowy scene as No 7 *Tom Rolt* heads an up train away from Dolgoch towards Nant Gwernol. *David Mitchell*

Quarry Siding

QUARRY SIDING: Driver Malcolm Brown eases his up train through the first set of points at Quarry Siding. The loco is No 4 *Edward Thomas*. *David Mitchell*

QUARRY SIDING: A double-headed down train passes the sleeper and rail stacks at Quarry Siding. *David Mitchell*

Right **QUARRY SIDING:** A lovely shot of No 7 *Tom Rolt* at Ceunant Coch, above Quarry Siding, with a very short vintage set. The smoke really adds to the atmosphere. *David Mitchell*

Left: **QUARRY SIDING:** No 1 *Talyllyn* (specially 'dirtied up' for the occasion) heads a photographic special past typical slate fencing between Quarry Siding and Abergynolwyn. *David Mitchell*

Abergynolwyn

Left: **Nr QUARRY SIDING:** Loco No 6, masquerading as *Duncan*, between Quarry siding and Abergynolwyn with Fireman Sarah Freeman watching the road ahead on 17 June 2006. *David Mitchell*

Above: **Nr QUARRY SIDING:** In a wintry scene, No 7 *Tom Rolt* heads a three-coach train up the valley between Quarry Siding and Abergynolwyn, seen from the B4405. *David Mitchell*

Above **ABERGYNOLWYN:** A very unusual photograph of *Dolgoch* at the head of its train on the down journey at Abergynolwyn station on 6 September 1991. *Robert Morland*

Right **ABERGYNOLWYN:** No 4 *Edward Thomas* waits to leave Abergynolwyn with a down train on 9 August 1961. *Norman Jones, TR collection*

ABERGYNOLWYN: Abergynolwyn station in about 1903. *Author's collection*

TR Collection

Above **ABERGYNOLWYN:** An early photo of No 3 *Sir Haydn* on a down train at Abergynolwyn, during the era when passenger service terminated here; the extension to Nant Gwernol was not completed until May 1976. *David Mitchell*

Left **ABERGYNOLWYN:** *Dolgoch* and its train stand in Abergynolwyn's west platform. *TR collection*

ABERGYNOLWYN: On Good Friday 2009 the TR held a 'Stations at Stations' event, which was a very innovative way of having the 'Stations of the Cross' – a traditional Good Friday devotion – on railway stations. Here the train travels up the loop at Abergynolwyn; Fireman James Foster is driving while Driver Bill Heynes keeps a look-out. *David Mitchell*

Nant Gwernol

Below left **NANT GWERNOL:** The first train to Nant Gwernol approaching journey's end on 22 May 1976. *TR collection*

Below **NANT GWERNOL:** No 2 *Dolgoch* heads a down photographic train away from Nant Gwernol, passing the site of the old winding house at the top of the incline down to Abergynolwyn village. The winding gear, the track through the now demolished winding house and the wagon turntable are all clearly visible. *TR collection*

NANT GWERNOL: A long-distance shot of No 2 *Dolgoch* at Nant Gwernol station. The photograph shows how the line is on a 'shelf' here, with the stream running down the ravine below. *David Mitchell*

NANT GWERNOL: No 3 *Sir Haydn* has arrived at Nant Gwernol on 12 June 2010. The loco will now uncouple and run round via the loop to the other end of the train to couple to the guard's van ready for the return journey. *David Mitchell*

Volunteers

DOLGOCH: The Talyllyn Railway would not exist today without a very dedicated band of volunteers. This early works train is driven by the late Bill Faulkner. No doubt Health and Safety rules would prevent the workers travelling on the wagons today! *David Mitchell*

ABERGYNOLWYN: The TR will happily host special occasions such as birthday parties and weddings. The author marked his 70th birthday with a special train followed by a buffet at King's Bistro at Wharf station. In this picture he is standing with his 5-month-old grandson Matthew and his elder son Justin, who has been a TR volunteer for 28 years and was the guard of the train. Three generations of the family! *Celia Adams*

PENDRE YARD: This photograph shows Guard and Blockman Gordon Rhodes with colleagues on 25 September 2010 at the end of the day on which he completed 50 years as a Traffic Volunteer (despite what the headboard says!). Driver Keith Foster is on the extreme right, and Fireman Andy Bailey on the footplate. *Author*

PENDRE YARD: Blockman Walter Crowe is at Pendre Blockpost on a lovely September afternoon waiting with the token he will exchange with Driver Keith Foster, who is driving an approaching up train from Wharf. In the headshunt is the flail mower, designed by John Bate and built in Pendre Works. *Author*

DOLGOCH FALLS: Long-standing volunteer Dale Coton tries out the new 'finger board' he has made for Dolgoch station. The person in charge of the station changes the board before each train enters the station so that passengers can see the destination. *David Mitchell*

ABERGYNOLWYN: An up train headed by No 2 *Dolgoch* makes its way to Nant Gwernol from Abergynolwyn above the village church dedicated to the patron saint of Wales, St David. This location is known on the TR as 'Amen Corner'! *David Mitchell*

TYWYN WHARF MUSEUM: On 4 April 2005 the late Bishop of Bangor (the Rt Rev Tony Crockett) paid an official visit to the TR, and on that day it was arranged that all the volunteers operating the railway had church or chapel connections. He acted as guard on the 1.55pm departure from Wharf, and later transferred to the footplate. He is seen here in the 'mock-up' of Rev Wilbert Awdry's study in the Wharf Museum, standing in front of the picture of the 'Isle of Sodor', the home of the railways in Wilbert's many books beloved by children (of all ages!). *Author's collection*

TYWYN WHARF: The TR presented Bishop Tony with a special loco headboard to mark his visit, which had pride of place in the Bishop's House until his untimely death from cancer in June 2008 at the age of 64. Here he is with the crew of his train: Driver Jonathan Mann, Guard Nigel Adams (who is himself ordained), Assistant Guard Bob Hey and Fireman Andy Vick. *Author's collection*

BRYNGLAS: The present Bishop of Bangor, the Rt Rev Andrew John, paid an official visit to the TR for a footplate trip on 7 June 2010, and the TR presented him with a loco headboard, as they had with his predecessor, Bishop Tony Crockett. He so enjoyed his footplate trip that he came back for a 'Driver Experience' train on 11 August 2010, and was asked to bring the headboard with him. He drove the engine for two trips under the guidance of Driver Mike Green, who is a church bellringer. He and the crew are seen in Brynglas loop waiting for a down passenger train to pass. *Barbara Fuller*

Above **ABERGYNOLWYN:** Bishop Andrew John was also invited to take part in the 'Stations at Stations' event on Good Friday 2009. Here he is seen in the guard's van with Guard Nigel Adams (an Anglican priest), Ian Drummond (a Baptist minister) and Clare Evans (daughter of Ian Evans, an Anglican reader). It was Ian who had the idea of having this innovative liturgy on the TR. It was repeated in 2010 and was also planned for Good Friday 2011. *David Mitchell*

Main picture **PENDRE:** A superb shot of loco No 1 Talyllyn (minus its cab) standing at Pendre with a photographic special on 16 March 2007. Fireman Andrew Thomas has been left in charge of the engine.

TYWYN WHARF: At the end of the day's operations on 23 August 2007 the TR had a 'photoshoot' with every loco in the yard at Wharf. The author – who was Duty Controller on that day – is the person in the blue shirt between the flail mower and loco No 2. *David Mitchell, TR collection*

TYWYN WHARF: No 1 *Talyllyn* stands on the coal road at Wharf, in front of No 2 *Dolgoch*. Driver Julian Stow is about to get on his engine. *David Mitchell*

Above right **PENDRE:** A rear view of No 1 *Talyllyn*, without its cab, just on the east side of Pendre level crossing gates ready for a test run. *Author*

Above far right **PENDRE:** A view of the footplate of the cabless No 1. *David Mitchell*

Right **PENDRE YARD:** No 3 *Sir Haydn* in Pendre yard. *Both TR collection*

Right **PENDRE YARD:** No 5 *Midlander* stands outside the south shed in Pendre yard with van No 6. This loco has now been totally rebuilt and refurbished. *TR collection*

Belowt **PENDRE YARD:** No 2 *Dolgoch* at Pendre: note the typical 'clutter' so familiar in loco yards and so important for modellers of such scenes. *Author*

Below right **DOLGOCH FALLS:** No 4 *Edward Thomas*, fitted with a Giesl ejector, leaves Dolgoch Falls on its way to Abergynolwyn on 9 August 1961. *Norman Jones, TR collection*

Left **PENDRE SHED** A superb shot of No 6 *Douglas* framed in the loco shed entrance at Pendre. *David Mitchell*

Right **PENDRE YARD:** 'Irish Pete' – better known to the TR now as No 7 *Tom Rolt* – in the early days of its rebuilding at Pendre. *TR collection*

Below **TYWYN WHARF:** Driver Julian Stow supervises his fireman filling loco No 7 *Tom Rolt* with water at Wharf station. *TR collection*

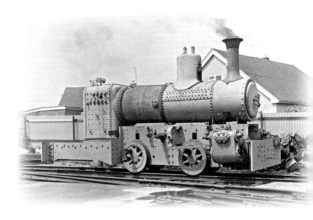

Top left **PENDRE YARD:** No 8 *Merseysider* stands in the yard loop at Pendre at the head of an engineering train; the trolley *Toby* stands in the loco yard. *Author*

Left **PENDRE YARD:** No 8 was rebuilt in the early part of the 21st century and here it stands outside the west carriage shed in its new appearance and livery. *Author*

Above **TYWYN WHARF:** No 9 *Alf*, named after Sir Alf Robens (Chairman of the National Coal Board at the time the loco was obtained from the NCB), is on the middle road at Wharf station in the process of loading loco No 4 *Edward Thomas* onto the low-loader ready to be lent to the Corris Railway. *TR collection*

Right **PENDRE YARD:** No 10 *Bryn Eglwys* stands down the 'back road' at Pendre with a works train. *TR collection*

Top right **BRYNGLAS:** The TR's trolley, *Toby*,

stands with the fire tender in the siding at Brynglas. When the weather has been dry for a long time, there is a risk of a loco setting fire to the grass at the trackside. Normally the crew spot the fire, stop and extinguish it. In prolonged dry spells, provision is made for the fire tender to follow a train through the Pendre-Brynglas section as a precaution, although this is very rarely done. The trolley has been repainted blue since this photograph was taken in 1992. *Author*

Rolling stock

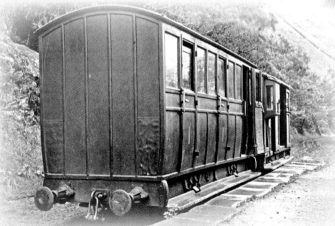

Above **TYWYN WHARF:** Young volunteer Phil Eaton sits on the end of a rake of slate wagons parked in the loop at Wharf station. He is the guard of a special train to include these wagons, which is being made up. *David Mitchell*

Right **ABERGYNOLWYN:** This lovely but undated picture shows a TR coach and a TR van (No 5) at Abergynolwyn. *Author's collection*

Above left **TYWYN WHARF:** Van No 5 at Wharf. *TR collection*

Above **BRYNGLAS:** The rear of an up train on its way to Nant Gwernol. When it reaches its destination the loco will run round and bring the stock back to Wharf station. *David Mitchell*

TYWYN WHARF: Glyn Valley Tramway coach No 14 stands at Wharf station, newly refurbished and painted. It was rescued by the TR many years ago from use as a garden shed! *TR collection*

Index

When visiting the railway...

The Railway Shop

The Railway Shop at Tywyn Wharf Station stocks a wide selection of transport and historic related items as well as Talyllyn Railway branded goods, Welsh items, Welsh crystal, maps, videos, books, gift confectionery, jewellery, jigsaws, occasion cards and many other items.